AF250237

Copyrighted Material

Boompop: An Introduction
Copyright © 2020 by Rod Goelz, Musicshare Publications, All Rights Reserved

No part of this publication may be reproduced, stored in a retrieval system, or transmitted, in any form or by any means--electronic, mechanical, photocopying, recording, or otherwise--without prior written permission from the publisher, except for the inclusion of brief quotation for review.

For information about this title or to order any other books and/or electronic media, contact the publisher.

Musicshare Publications
rod@rodgoelz.com
www.rodgoelz.com

ISBN: 978-0-578-63805-8

Printed in the United States of America

Cover design by Michael S. Males of Sunken Treasure Design
www.sunkentreasuredesign.com

Boompop: An Introduction

BOOMPOP

An Introduction

Rod Goelz

Dedication

This book is memory of my family: Edward Goelz (Father), Louise Goelz (Mother), and Robert Goelz (Brother).

I think about you all every day.

Acknowledgments

The author wishes to thank the following people who made *Boompop/An Introduction* possible: my late parents Edward & Louise Goelz, Scott Anderson, Cal Weary (Weary Arts Group), the late Douglass Knight, Andrew Gobel, Abbie Sealover, Rosanna DiSebastiano, Michael Males (Sunken Treasure Design), Greg Swenson, Roy Smith, Mike Drayer, Adam McAllister, Dave Pedrick (Working Musician Podcast), Simon Overmiller, Pastor Joel Folkemer and Carla Christopher (at Union Lutheran Church/York, PA), Crispus Attucks (York, PA), James Klippel, Todd Bedard. This book would not have been possible if not for the care and diligence of Kara Davis who edited every word and kept me on track. I am forever indebted.

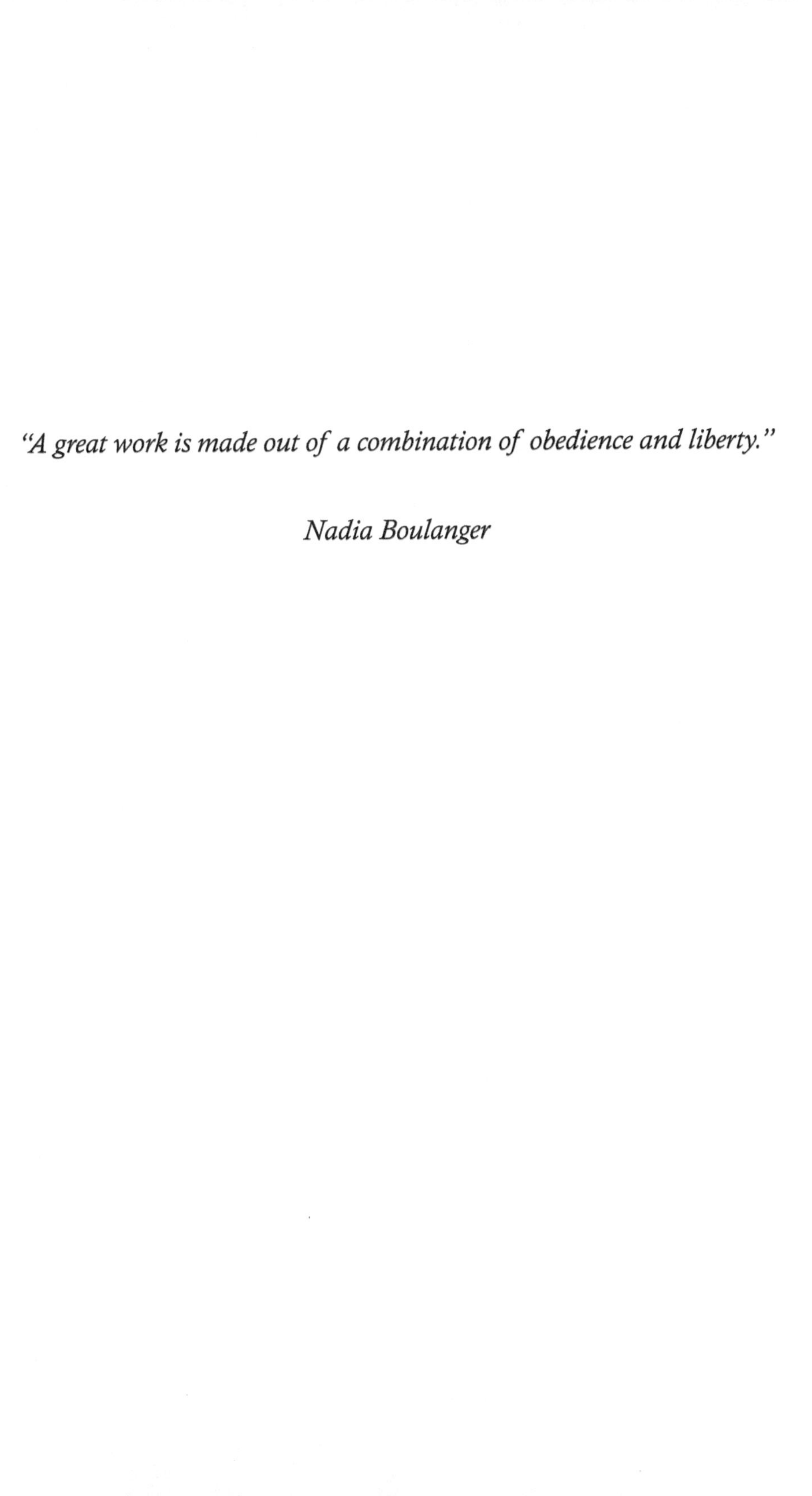

"A great work is made out of a combination of obedience and liberty."

Nadia Boulanger

Table of Contents

Forward

Music is the blood that feeds the brain, heart, and soul of human experience. At its core there is a cadence driving beats and vibration into rhythmic sensation. A universal language of the anointed and blessed tuning forks of the universe.

We are the chosen few that see in notes, and note what we see. Reporting to the world about itself through sound's organized anarchy. We eat and starve by measure at the table of life and pound out drum licks in solid wood to make hips sway and bend.

There is a BOOM!! In the distance bending trees and twisting rays of light into particles. Broken down, we see music in its most basic form...raw drenched in funk and sharp edges.

Reach out and POP!!! It gets into you. It resets your internal click track and sets you to Alpha Centauri mean time. A call and response with the alien in your closet and the monster under your bed. BOOM!!! POP!!! BOOM!!! POP!!!

The stars are not the limit here.

Cal Weary
Weary Arts Group/CEO

Introduction

Who Is This Book For?

I'm often asked, "What Is Boompop?" To those people that ask, this book is for you. You are the immediate audience. My approach to teaching, playing, or conceptualizing music has never been written about in a complete form. Part of this book will be about, "what is Boompop?" The other part is about the deeper building blocks that went into its conception-musical concepts mainly.

I believe my approach will make any improvisation musician a well rounded musician, capable of tackling any musical obstacle. Boompop, in part, is a set of survival skills. More than that, it opens many artistic doors. Suddenly all colors of music are available and ready to be explored. Boompop is more than a musical approach or style. We are more alike than we are different. We all breathe the same air. We all benefit from learning from one another, both culturally and musically.

Lastly, this book is for the music educator. I believe my ideas to be sound. They have produced many fine musicians of all types over the last 30 years. Boompop gives many more concepts to play with. Improvisation without elitism is what is offered. We take all styles in our quest of musical discovery. We are students of time, melody, harmony, and culture. The sky's the limit to what is possible with Boompop in your musical toolbox.

Why I'm Writing This Book

The story of Boompop is also my story. I've been an educator for 30+ years, a musician for over 40 years. I've played with every kind of musician imaginable. I never shy away from an experience. I saw how certain approaches and beliefs in music presented severe limitations that I, myself, was not comfortable with. While some musician's style can be built off their limitations, the educator in me saw that style should come from possibilities, not limitations. That energy shift made all the difference to my approach in music.

My earliest memories are singing along to Beach Boy and Beatle 45s. I was singing to the radio before I could read. Music and musical expression has been a central theme in my life. I've been down and out, like most anyone else, but never really alone. Music, to me, is the hidden language of the transcendent. It gives us a connection to everything.

I've learned and experienced a lot in my lifetime. As I get older, I realize that very few people have been in the position that my life has afforded me. Day after day, I put in my time as a musician, as a composer, as a teacher—chasing the subjects I'm so curious and passionate about. Boompop is the culmination of these efforts. Conceptualizing the craft of music—listening, performing, and organizing for artistic gains! Boompop is the bigger picture. It is my hope that it will also change the way you see the world.

Before we get started consider this quote:

"The finest musicians have a floor below which their playing never falls: the floor of their musical house. When confronted with the most unbelievable performance obstacles… they still manage to play well, if not brilliantly. The trick is to raise that floor level possible, and to keep it there. Let's look at your musical house. It can have as many rooms and be furnished in any way you like. Some would build their house in a classical style filled solely with classical furnishings: a Beethoven foyer, a Debussy living room, a Mozart den. Others might choose to build a 'house of blues.' As with any home, the style and furnishings reflect you interests and tastes. In my opinion, the musical houses are the most eclectic-a jazz kitchen, a rock & roll rec room, maybe an R&B bedroom. Of course, mixing it up would make the hippest house of all."

Scott Ambush / Spyro Gyra

Part One: The Language of Boompop

What is Boompop?

*"For a wide range of expression,
you need the biggest pool of knowledge."*

Edgar Meyer

For those that ask, "What Is Boompop?" In short, it is my approach to music as well as a creative philosophy. In Boompop, groove takes center stage; it is our #1 tool. Boompop is an approach that values improvisation and open minded musical expression. Boompop musicians borrow from every style. Boompop is not a fully formed style or classical form. Most styles have found their sound—Jazz, Blues, Rock, etc. Boompop is "how we do what we do", an approach that aims for no definitive sound—rather the approach and attitude by which those sounds were created. All styles make use of rhythm and groove. Therefore, there is something to be learned from all styles.

Improvisation is nothing new in music education. Boompop musicians study all kinds of improvised music—Rock, Funk, HipHop, Blues, R&B, Jazz, Latin, Country, Bluegrass, Gospel, etc. There is never a shortage of material to take influence in! Improvisation is a survival skill for Boompop musicians. It helps us adapt to any musical situation.

Movement and Vibe are vital tools in the Boompop toolbox. eurhythmics, or the body movement, and popular music can be taught and learned with students as young as three. They learn to feel music and not fear music. It is pure joyful expression, but learning and conditioning is happening. Vibe is the feeling behind the attitude, style, and enthusiasm. What something sounds like goes deeper than just the notes we play. It's in the motion of the body, the sting in the notes we play, the sincerity, tenacity, the musical grease, or the sweetness we are trying to express.

Boompop explores the heightened benefits of rhythm and it's through this pursuit that so many other things become heightened and possible—improvisation, adaptation, accompaniment, and communication.

The Boompop Learning Family

*"If you don't go out and gather experiences,
you'll have nothing to bring back to your music."*

Steve Bailey

Stated simply: Less experienced musicians will progress quicker when accompanied by musicians that have more experience. We try to provide learning experiences that all musical levels benefit from. More experienced members of the family share advice and playtime with the less experienced kin. In our family, it's less about competition and more about collaboration with people of various skill levels. Boompop teachers find ways of making the musical encounters mutually beneficial, creating performances and opportunities that require different skill levels.

The Good Teacher

A good music teacher is a perpetual student of the craft, the passion that is music making. If the learning stops at any point, so does the teacher's effectiveness and vitality. Music is discovery. Music is about taking chances when creating and not having to be perfect in this quest. Teachers who are students of many different musical languages and styles of groove make great Boompop teachers. Boompop is a comparative approach to learning music. Music style is the exploration of musical variables. Styles may vary in the way they use rhythm, for example, but all styles make use of rhythm. For this reason, we study all styles.

Boompop's Idea of Good Music

We find meaning in all kinds of music. Some musicians find their sound by applying limits to their listening and influence. However, it is our philosophy that if you limit your listening, you limit the creative ingredients you develop music with. When people prefer to create within limits it defines their sound. Their power comes from limitation and is often not open to other styles to support their stance. Boompop explores the variations and combinations of music, the varied musical colors and textures.

Survival Skills

"Research your own experience; Absorb what is useful;
Reject what is useless; Add what is specifically your own."

Bruce Lee

We teach survival skills. What it takes to survive depends on what level you are on. For the beginner to survive enthusiasm must be maintained, belief must be instilled. They must have early success experiences, basic motor skills must be developed, basic practice habits must be established, basic musical understanding must be understood, and a relationship with music must be encouraged and fostered.

The Ground Rhythm

The Ground Rhythm is the internal pulse within a song that determines tempo and feel. It is the rhythm that moves through our bodies as we listen to and play music. Body movement and good rhythm skills are undeniably linked. The study of this system is called "eurhythmics"—meaning "good rhythm". Think of eurhythmics as a musical gym class. It's a fact, if you don't move to the rhythm as you're playing your instrument, your rhythm will suffer.

The Ground Rhythm isn't busy or cluttered. It's solid as a rock.

Start by tapping your foot to the beat. Determining this quarter note pulse within any given song or groove is your first step towards mastering its rhythm. Have you noticed when attending a concert the audience collectively moves to the rhythm of the music? This is the ground rhythm. The fact that the audience moves to this pulse illustrates that this musical instinct is within most of us. How we decorate the space within the ground rhythm determines our phrasing. The practice of movement within music, also known as eurhythmics, helps us feel the pulse, which is essential for good rhythm.

In the past, music teachers had their students tap their foot to keep good rhythm. In Boompop, foot tapping is for sissies. The Rule For Good Rhythm is as follows: When you feel the musical pulse within a song you're working on moving your body to the the pulse! Don't just move your feet; move your upper body, your arms, head, and shoulders, etc. The groove must have an internal connection which requires various kinds of movement. Look at your favorite musicians as they perform—music, movement, and performance all comes together.

"Groove is the Center.
"Play the rests. The notes will take care of themselves."

Anonymous

Most music has a groove of some sort. Until that musical flow occurs and is experienced, learning feels like an exercise. Groove is central to all contemporary music. It can be approached on both basic and advanced levels, and its understanding and application is one of the key educational goals in my teaching—building skills with groove as a foundational tool all other musical disciplines can be more effectively addressed. The experience of groove is not dependent upon mastery of reading music—simple rhythmic understanding is sufficient to get started.

A groove relies on predictability, repetition, and a strong melody. Is everything on the grid? As James Brown has often mentioned, all his band members are drummers regardless of the physical instrument they play. They are all part of the musical weave. What this means is our job is to play using rhythms that enhance the central groove. So think like a drummer!

A last important note about groove and arranging is the understanding that at any given moment within a groove there are supporting roles and lead roles. Lead roles are more musically active; Larry Graham's bass line on Sly And The Family Stone's "Thank You (Falettinme Be Mice Elf Agin)," for example. This lead role is busy, but still pocket. In order for this groove to work it relies on the supporting roles. Many grooves are made up of only supporting roles. When lead roles make an appearance, they require support to make the sound musically cohesive.

What is "The Pocket"?

The Pocket is about making good musical choices. It's about learning to play good rhythms and good phrases. It's about listening to your mates and playing the right notes, rhythms, and phrases to push the groove forward. Every style has a pocket that musicians strive and thrive within. To be able to play pocket helps in establishing musical taste—the "what is necessary to make this song pop" quotient. To play pocket, you have to be aware of your musical surroundings and make good choices accordingly. Too many notes, showboating, or bad phrasing results in the act of sound littering! Don't litter, nobody is impressed with too many notes. Rather, littering serves as an annoyance and nobody will want to play with you.

In a groove, sometimes we have an active part, sometimes we have a supporting role. It's important to know the difference. Active parts are lots of notes, sometimes with syncopated rhythms. The rule is an easy one—the active part must be supported with less notes and solid rhythms. Do not compete with that active part as it needs your support to carry it forward. Musical Anecdote: Prince would yell "chicken grease" to his support guitar player, which meant lay down a solid 16th groove. Prince worked pocket syncopated magic guitar wizardry over top that "chicken grease."

The Two Musical Disciplines:
Jazz vs. Classical

More than styles of music, these are ways of conceptualizing, practicing, and playing music. The Classical discipline is about respecting and recreating that which came before. This discipline is about capturing the notes, vibe, and nuances of a work—no matter what style.

The Jazz discipline deals with experimentation and improvisation. In fact, improvisation is often described as, "composition sped up in real time." These are skills that anyone can learn. This type of musician practices aiming for a different set of skills that allow for the musician to go beyond the song, recording, or score.

Boompop musicians love the Jazz discipline—that's their wheelhouse, but in reality both jazz and classical disciplines must be used. Core skills, technique, and vocabulary come from replicating what happened before. Learning to repurpose these lessons are what the jazz discipline offers. Once the musician has amassed some technique and vocabulary, exploration and improvisation becomes the next goal. To be able to speak the language, not simply memorize someone else's interpretation of that language.

Range Of Expression:
Musical Aesthetics

The philosophy of aesthetics concerns itself with notions such as what is beautiful and what is ugly. Aesthetics is not just beauty for the sake of beauty. It is also the underlying principle and guiding force behind the music—music as a means of expressing some inner personal truth. Is there room for ugly in musical expression? The answer is yes! If you compose a piece that speaks about racial inequality, you may choose dissonance, as it best represents the texture of the spoken word. Dissonant rhythms, chord changes, melody, and playing styles all play an important role in selling the storyline.

Part Two: Boompop Tools

The Study Of Riddims

We'll define riddims as a rhythm section motif. The two to four measure groove and all its individual pieces—guitar, bass, drums, keys, percussion, melodies, and rhythms. The study of riddims is a study of how the pieces fit together. The lessons gained from this are endless.

For the Boompop musician, the riddim is an essential learning tool. We study riddims in every style. Motown, AC/DC, Marley, James Brown, Stax, Blue Note, The Beatles, and Chess—the riffs to Enter Sandman, the three guitar force of The Funk Brothers, Chicago, New Orleans, Philadelphia, Kingston, and London. Riddims exist in every culture, every style of music and collect experiences from every culture.

Movement And Music/Eurhythmics

Before I knew much about music, I knew music and movement were unequivocally linked. If I didn't move a certain way, I would be unable to play a certain passage with good articulation. And without which that part would die. Further, movement is linked to good rhythm, the whole body is involved with good rhythm. Movement often inspires enthusiasm, bringing the celebration, and instills fearlessness. College has taught me there's a word and movement within the musical pursuit. It's called eurhythmics.

Movement can be taught to the youngest of children. I have experience with classes of students as young as 3 years old and it is a vital part of the Boompop experience. Boompop music teachers are inventive in the ways they integrate movement into the discipline of music.

Articulation & Nuance

Articulation deals with the infinite ways we can play a note, strike a string, hit a drum, etc. Hard, soft, short, connected—each with infinite variables. The style of technique also influences how we articulate a note. These are the nuances that make music more like the act of painting. It's not just the notes that are played, it is in the finer points of how those notes are played. Similar to the shades of color in a painting, the notes and how they are played are the shades within a melody.

What are other nuances within music?

The Verbal Cadence

The Verbal Cadence makes rhythms and sounds so much easier to translate. The easiest of all is the four quarter note drum sound, Boom-Pop-Boom-Pop, for example. Traditional musical education spells out Ta and Ti-Ti—in what is referred to as stick figure notation. Jazz Icon Clark Terry created "Doodle Tonguing" to help in the aid of learning to improvise. Beatboxing is a form of verbal cadence. Boompop educators make use of the verbal cadence whenever possible.

The Grid

"The heart of a music is its rhythm. The heart of rhythm section music is the rhythm."

Wynton Marsalis

The Grid is a visual concept of the pocket, which is how the Boompop musician keeps track of rhythm, the groove, and their place in the mix. Further, The Grid is a way of interpreting musical time, pocket, note usage, the importance of space within music. It is a way of seeing where all the notes fit in a particular riddim, groove or song. Whole, half, quarter, 8th, and 16th note rhythms and rests (in their infinite combinations) can all be placed on The Grid. The Grid has a visual component. It looks like this:

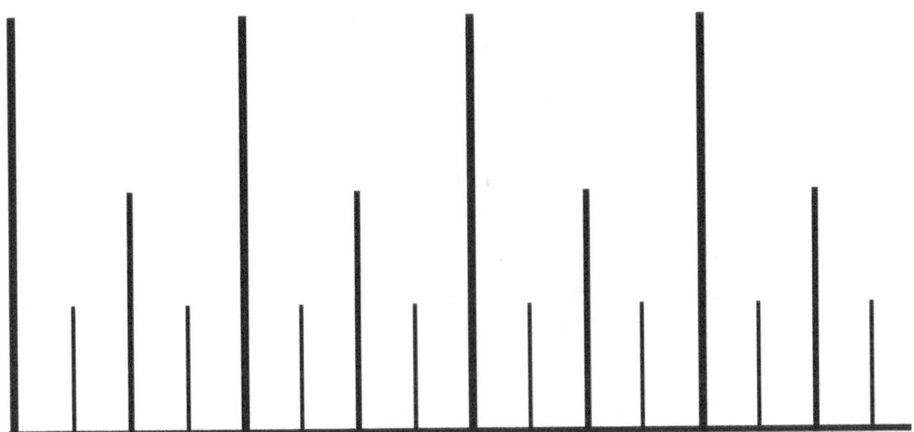

The Genesis of Boompop

"The only element of jazz that I keep is improvisation."

Jan Garbarek

Somewhere along the line, jazz became a classical artform. Rules were established that limited the possibility for growth. Jazz was meant to be the sound of freedom. Over the years, this freedom crystallized into something more structured. When you think of the word Jazz there is a sound that comes to mind—a preferable sound to all other sounds, according to some people's tastes. Further, other sounds won't be considered if they run too far outside of this musical paradigm. In this way, jazz has become a classical form—freedom within the confines the art has set for itself, but not freedom.

Styles, by their nature, have borders. These are qualities that define and classify them. Boompop can take many forms, sound wise. It is the approach and attitude with which the music was conceived. The differences between the fiddle and violin lie in how it's conceived and conceptualized—that's Boompop. No borders, no boundaries.

The Musical Concept of Repurposing

*"All forms are complex once you get to a really high level, and jazz and hip-hop
are so connected. In hip-hop, you sample, while in jazz, you take Broadway
tunes and turn them into something different. They're both forms that repurpose other forms of music."*

Kamasi Washington

To repurpose means to find new uses for the tools we are given.
For the musician, it is this concept that helps us build improvisational
vocabularies exponentially. All learning should be approached with repurposing in mind. Musical licks without an understanding of how to
apply that lick is wasteful and ineffective. It's critical to learn how to
apply that lick in other situation keeping in mind the key center and musical color. When we learn another person's music, we are not just learning a collection of isolated songs, techniques, riffs, solos, and the like.
Rather, we need to learn the concept of the idea so that we may speak
freely without restriction—like natural thoughts and ideas or words in
a conversation. Understand that by not learning the bigger picture, the
concept behind a musical idea, you are choosing to limit yourself. Learn
that solo, but learn to repurpose it.

Boompop Concept of Fusion

*"My definition of hip hop is taking elements from many other spheres of
music to make hip hop. Whether it be breakbeat, whether it be the groove and
grunt of James Brown or the pickle-pop sounds of Kraftwerk or Yellow Magic
Orchestra, hip hop is also part of what they call hip-house now, or trip hop, or
even parts of drum n' bass."*

Afrika Bambaataa

Fusion simply means mixing of styles and it is usually associated with improvisational art forms. Like the alchemist in the laboratory,
unique expression comes from mixtures. The original fusion that Miles
Davis conceptualized when he created his "Bitches Brew" was thought

to be a mixture of Jazz and Rock. The mixture of styles is the secret sauce within Boompop—any style can theoretically bring new life to an existing style. This vision expands on the original definition of fusion—rock mixing with jazz, funk mixing with jazz, etc. In Boompop, the mixing of styles leads to denser, more original ideas and sounds. It is with this mindset that originality can happen.

Music As Communication

"Music is the major form of communication. It's the commonest vibration, the people's news broadcast, especially for kids."

Richie Havens

When people get together and play music, many actions and activities take place. First of all they share space! They communicate with people in the same space as they are in. In a world that is increasingly more digital, communication has come to mean social media, texting, gaming, email, maybe a phone call here and there. This has already changed the world in ways we can't predict and will continue to do so. Our abilities to cope, thrive, and enjoy personal human interaction are at risk. Face to face communication could be considered quaint. The digital age has changed us, this is certain.

Performed music is a language of what could become a bygone era. Musicians communicate every time they come together in the most meaningful ways. They listen to each other and respond accordingly. They compromise for the good of the groove, the whole, and it feels right to do so. They speak a language that transcends written or even spoken language. It leaves them feeling the spirit—an energy that lasts for days. Performing improvised music is like the perfect democracy. Race or social status is of no concern on the bandstand. Can you hang? That's all we care about. We support, we willingly compromise for the better of the whole. Sometimes we lead, while others support us, but nobody loses.

Part Three: Practice

Practice vs. Play

"When practicing, it's great to break a part down into its different elements, start slowly, and then try to build up the speed until you're playing as fast as you possibly can."

Synyster Gates

Practice and play are equal partners in acquiring any kind of lasting motor skill. Practice requires discipline because we are working on weakness, which is less fun than play. Once the thing we are practicing can be placed into a groove, that discipline becomes play. Play doesn't take discipline because it's fun. Playing for long hours makes us better, obviously, for it applies what we learned in practice. The better we get at practice, the less time we have to spend doing it because that skill is more developed.

Boompop instructors start by assessing strengths and weaknesses. Some musicians are singers, others have great ears, and some have physical dexterity. Whatever the strengths may be they can be used to address weaknesses, helping to build them up.

Discipline 1: Vibing

vibe: informal : a distinctive feeling or quality capable of being sensed

Active practice through active imitation. This involves imitating the groove, rhythm, phrasing, articulation, sound, attitude, etc. Imitating the overall vibe of the music. Imitating note choice is somewhat important, but more important is how those notes are organized—which scale and how that scale can be used in practical situations.

In the process, you will be making big strides building musical vocabulary, groove memory, and organic technique—the sound of effortlessness. The act of vibing emphasizes listening and imitation skills. The act of vibing can be used in practice as well as performance. Those who vibe consider it to be the most pleasurable form of practice as it feels remarkably like play. Eyes shut, dig into the groove, notes, attitude, and sound of your favorite music and players, and imitate. The more you practice vibing the better you get at it! Vibing works in all styles and for all kinds of players, from Chuck Berry, Wes Montgomery, John Coltrane, Herbie Hancock and all people/instruments, styles, and sounds in between!

Discipline 2: Mining

"A good composer does not imitate; he steals."

Igor Stravinsky

Boompop musicians often practice by mining other musicians for ideas. Like miners who mine for coal, diamonds, etc. We borrow concepts in our practice and work to repurpose them. We mine for many things. We mine the different rhythm languages, styles of groove, melody and melodic approaches, riffs, licks, chord approaches, different types of progressions, and comping approaches within the set chord changes. We'll even mine for ideas on arranging. Any part of the music making process is fertile ground for mining. When mining, concepts can be just as important as notes, chords, and sounds. It is through this act of scouring through recorded history that we grow as musicians. It is then that we find out what is possible.

Musical Physics & Economy Of Motion/ Perpetual Motion Concept

"...an object in motion, stays in motion..."

Sir Isaac Newton

Economy of Motion principals deal with working smarter not harder in our practice. There are countless examples of this a good teacher can provide. It can be as simple correct bowing, guitar players strumming and picking, drummers practice rudiments with economy of motion in mind.

The physical act of playing relies on consistent limb/digit movement without unnecessary starts and stops. The starts and stops are lapses in rhythm; lapses that mess up the groove. Each instrument has its own way with dealing with this "perpetual motion" concept.

Economy Of Motion Tip: When guitar players strum, they keep your arm in constant motion at all times, even within the silence of the strumming pattern. This keeps the groove tight, devoid of starts and stops. Determine how this principle can be applied to your chosen instrument.

Passive Listening

"The simplest way of listening to music is to listen for the sheer pleasure of the musical sound itself. That is the sensuous plane. It is the plane on which we hear music without thinking, without considering it in any way."

Aaron Copeland

Passive listening is what most people do. It's pure enjoyment without any thought or restrictions. Music moves you or it doesn't. Musicians can learn from this mindset on some level. It is a reminder that there are no guilty pleasures when listening to music. Just pleasures.

Active Listening

"What we hear is the quality of our listening."

Robert Fripp

Active listening is what musicians do. It takes into account musical ideas such a groove, instrumentation, melody, chord changes, nuance, arrangement, storyline within the lyrics, production, etc. All play a role in how a musician hears music.

The Boompop learning curve is mostly about listening. We try not to be too critical as there is much to learn in all music. We learn in three ways: 1) by taking in and absorbing the music the first time we listen; 2) Then we imitate what we hear; 3) And finally, with the aid of music theory, we learn to repurpose the concept in a multitude of ways and in a multitude of styles—assimilating the concepts into our own musical language. Improvising melodic musicians (sax, guitar, etc.) mine other improvisers for melodic content—what can be taken from the music? Rhythm section partners mine for different grooves, voice leading, comping styles, and riddim combinations. We pick up all the important nuances by listening and listening alone. Some musicians feel guilty because of the importance we place on listening. In Boompop, there is no guilt in listening because it is through listening that musical innovation happens. Capisce?

"Ears are made not for hearing but for listening. Listening is an active skill, whereas hearing is passive. Listening is something that we have to work at - it's a relationship with sound. And yet, it's a skill that none of us are taught."

Julian Treasure

Exercise: Listening the song "The River" by Bruce Springsteen. Try not to make any judgements. You don't need to be a fan of "the boss" to learn something from him. Check out the arrangement. What instruments do you hear? Are there interesting choices of instruments? Check out the storyline. Who is telling the story? What in the musical arrangement of the song corresponds with the storyline and the characters of the story. What about the rhythm section (guitar, bass, drums, piano, etc)? How would you describe the type of comping on the track?

Part Four: Melody

What is a Melody?

"There's a melody in everything. And once you find the melody, then you connect immediately with the heart."

Carlos Santana

A melody is the singable component within music. Anything that can be sung is said to be melodic. Boompop musicians are students of melody. They will seek it out and learn from it. Any form of melody is worth studying and incorporating, but we take melody one step further. We try to organize it for improvisational purposes. Tonesets are an introductory tool that Boompop students learn about and make use of in their practice.

What is a Motif?

A motif can be defined as, "a short succession of notes producing a single impression; a brief melodic or rhythmic formula out of which longer passages are developed." These are the smallest of musical blocks—out of which greater things become possible.

"My greatest inspiration has always been singers--they have the ability to get personal..." Jaco Pastorius

Tool Box: Tonesets

As I mentioned, any form of melody is worth studying and incorporating, but in Boompop, we take melody one step further. We try to organize it for improvisational purposes. Tonesets are an introductory tool that Boompop students learn about and make use of in their practice.

In the Boompop toolbox is something referred to as a toneset.

A toneset is a collection of notes organized for ease in improvisation. Tonesets are a simpler way of conceptualizing melodic choices when improvising. They are more compact than scales and are unique to the Boompop discipline.

Let's begin our study of tonesets by starting with two fundamental patterns, the major and minor tonesets. They are organized by scale degrees. In organizing these patterns we pay attention to scale degrees that are unique to that specific toneset. The Major toneset makes use of the first, second, fifth and sixth scale degrees of a major scale. Rather than using a traditional scale, just use these important notes—1 2 5 6—over Major and Dominant sounds.

Exercise: Improvise the Major Toneset intervals over a G/C/D chord progression using the G Major Toneset (see Youtube).

The Minor toneset consists of the fourth, fifth, flat seventh, and first scales degrees.

Exercise: Improvise the Minor Toneset intervals over a Ami7 to D7 chord progression using the A Minor Toneset (see Youtube).

What makes a good guitar solo?

"I don't like guitar solos that are like, 'Look at me, look at me!'
I like guitar solos that are little songs within the songs."

Taylor Hawkins

Melody is the number one ingredient! Even the flashy guitar solo has to have a melodic core. The soloist must have an understanding of phrases. Otherwise, you're just noodling. Be able to play in key and have a toolbox for each of the tonal colors—major, minor, and dominant. Flashy playing is nice, as everybody loves a virtuoso, but do right by the song.

What about Minor and Dominant sounds and chords? Use this pattern: 4 5 b7 1.

Explore in all keys across your instrument. Super simple! This improvisational tool is MAGIC!

Part Five: Harmony and Chords

What Are Chords/Chord Changes?

"There, in the chords and melodies, is everything I want to say. The words just jolly it along. It's always been my way of expressing what, for me, is inexpressible by any other means."

David Bowie

A defining feature of modern music is the advent of chord changes. They existed before, but weren't nearly as prevalent before 1900. Then along came W.C. Handy and his 12-Bar Blues invention. Chords became the support for the melody—a sonic support. This innovation was a huge shift from what came before. Once W.C. Handy's innovation took off, chords and melody were inseparable!

Chords were once only thought of as notes or voices grouped together—one on top another—three or more. The big shift was grouping chords together in a progression as a means to support a single melody. Boompop musicians are students of the many ways chords can be organized from style to style.

Comping (Rhythm Section)

Comping is what great rhythm section players do. They take the basic chords of a song and come up with their own parts that take the song further musically. "Comp" comes from the word "accompany" and addresses the discipline of creating great music with limited resources (chord changes). To be a skilled accompanist you must have:

· A good knowledge of chords all over the neck. Different styles of music use different kinds of chords.

· Good rhythm—this is true for many things but especially comping.

· A good understanding of musical styles—every style of music has musical benchmarks that makes its style of comping unique.

· Diverse techniques—strumming, finger-style, pick-style, broken chording techniques.

· A good understanding of harmony—how chords and melody work.

Practice Comping:
The "One Chord Challenge"

Break out the drum machine and then pick a groove, key, and chord. See how far comping and creative skills take you. Your vocabulary will become apparent. The knowledge of how chord voicings, substitutions, double stops (two note voicings), and single ornamentation will become apparent. Next up "The Two Chord Challenge".

Three Types Of Tonality

All sounds within the Boompop universe can be organized more or less into three kinds of tonality: Major, Minor, and Dominant. This approach is simple but effective. Boompop students develop tool boxes for each of these tonalities. How does each style of music make use of this simplification? Chicago Blues, Rock, and Bebop each approach the three tonalities differently.

Part Six: The Importance of the Blues

The Importance of The Blues

*"The only way to create something new today
is to know what happened yesterday."*

Chuck Rainey

W.C. Handy was the creator of the 12 bar blues chord progression. For this reason alone he is the most influential musician/composer of the twentieth century. His creation influenced all styles deeply—Jazz, Blues, Folk, Delta Blues, Swing, Bebop, Country, Race Music, Jump Blues, R&B, Rock n' Roll, Funk, Gospel, Heavy Metal, and Punk Rock. With the 12 Bar Blues, America found its sound and influences. The Blues music was America's music—no other place in the world where it could have been created—a metaphor for America itself.

The Blues changed the world in many ways, musically speaking:

- The structure of music became defined by the inter-relationship of chords and melody. No longer would it be defined as melodies intersecting.

- Music was a dance music—movement, celebration, culture and ritual are forever linked.

- With The Blues a musical stamp was created by the common folk, not by the wealthy and it represented the circumstances and tastes of the "common man."

- Musical ensembles were much smaller by necessity. Smaller groups were easier to maintain.

- The Blues came about through exploration and improvisation! The ability to improvise in these ensembles was a survival skill and it was this ability that gave The Blues its unique sound. The jam session gave birth to everything—new sounds and new combinations.

- The Blues brought about many repurposed instruments, including the drum set, upright bass, guitar, banjo, saxophone, harmonica, etc.

All of these instruments existed before, with the exception of the drum set, but the new music broadened the scope of what was possible.

- Blues melody emphasized the importance in emoting like the human voice—the notes in between the notes—the blue notes, the soulful howl, the grease!

- The Blues is responsible for the modern horn and rhythm sections and the function of musicians playing together, mostly without the aid of written music.

The Blues in Practice

The Boompop musician sees The Blues as the most useful learning tool there ever was for attaining musical freedom. The whole language of The Blues, in all its variations, is the musical laboratory of melody, chord, groove, and the infinite ways they can be combined. Your growth depends on your ability to make good use of this tool.

The Blues: What to Practice and How

- Practice all things to a jam track.

- View the organizational tools, like tonesets, scales, and arpeggios with a backing track. Play in key. Be able to play each of these patterns in key.

- Listen to other people often. Mine for melodies, motifs, and longer phrases. Sing them! Play them on your instrument with the backing track.

- Comping over all grooves. Make use of the drum machine. Swing, Rock, Funk, R&B, Jump Blues, Country, all styles. Make use of The Blues—The Blues is the unifying thread with all American music.

- Audiation—That "hear it before you play it" skill jazz musicians have. It turns out that this can be taught and learned.

Soloists: Stop practicing scales in the traditional way. Work on playing phrases within the scales. We learn to speak not by reading a dictionary, but in speaking sentences. Like the rhythm and pattern of words that make up a poem, music has in own rhythm and pattern which is referred to as prosody in the written word. This concept can be applied to musical patterns as well. A good approach to strengthen your prosody-related skills in improvisation is to focus on creating musical phrases, rather than playing scales. Scales are like the alphabet, they are not music in themselves. Experiment with creating short, singable phrases as you improvise, not merely playing scales.

Exercise: mine recorded blues for melodies, sing what you hear, find those melodies on your instrument. Sing like melodies, two notes phrases to start.

What Is Folk Music?

"A folk song is what's wrong and how to fix it."

Woody Guthrie

America has always been a melting pot of varying cultures—people who've come from all over the world and every walk of life. The many cultures' music and influences reflect this—from the fiddle tunes of Ireland, pipe songs of Scotland, syncopated rhythms, drums, and chants from Africa. This is the roots of American Folk Music as well as American music and is referred to as Roots Music. Just as The Blues is a rabbit hole worth exploring, so are the variations on fiddle tunes, folk melodies, chants, and rhythms which give us more insight on different styles of melody.

Folk music and songs represent the music of the people—normal people from all walks of life. These songs are singable and are created without the aid or knowledge of written notation rather than composed. These songs tell a story. Every culture has their own folk music—songs that define their experience in living. These are the ear worms that we take with us to bed each night. Everybody has their list of 2000 songs that define their experience. What are yours?

Part Seven: Boompop in the Classroom

What Does Boompop Teach Young Children (3 to 5 years old)?

The core lessons important to Boompop are learned naturally because of the "music as play" mindset. This approach removes the anxiety from the music making process and fosters fearless exploration. When Boompop has been implemented in a preschool setting it is introduced in a "music as play" approach that serves students throughout their musical life. Some of these benefits include:

- Learning not to fear music.

- A hands on experiences with musical instruments, playing rhythmically.

- Groove and rhythm. Prosody and language.

- Beginnings of reading and organizing music – 1234.

- Fearless singing and self esteem.

- First steps audiation—bringing out melodies from inside.

- First steps to improvisation—making use of the tools.

- History of song and composers.

The beauty of Boompop and music education of this type is that there are benefits that go beyond music. Some of these include problem solving skills, language development, communication, creativity, singing as self expression, courage to explore without fear, as well as providing benchmarks in history. Even bringing mathematics and organization into the creative realm--improvisation as well as arranging and composition.

What Does Boompop Teach The Rest Of Us?

For older musicians, BoomPop serves as a creative yet practical approach to conquering all contemporary music and related disciplines. You see, rhythm and groove are at the forefront of every contemporary style and groove are at the center of the BoomPop approach. The music as play mindset remains throughout all ages of learning BoomPop. The study of improvisation is vital. We borrow from all cultures and styles in our learning the freedom/responsibility improvisation presents. From Rock, Funk, Jazz, Swing, Metal, R&B, Reggae—the Riddim concept of Jamaica, the Raga of India, the drum circle interactions passed down from Africa, Native Americans, and Congo Square in New Orleans. Melody and accompaniment (comping) are equally important.

Another important facet of BoomPop is acquiring melodic and harmonic vocabulary from the icons of yesterday. We see value in note for noting. This gives the necessary raw musical material needed for informed improvisation to happen. We are students of melody and repurposing those melodies in everyday situations. To do this we utilize a readapted Suzuki-like approach (by ear/by rote) to learning melodies, riffs, licks, phrases, and solos. We also copy sounds--the sound of Jimi Hendrix, the sound of Maceo Parker, the sound of Louis Armstrong, etc. Vocabulary is essential, every student builds their own multi-faceted musical toolbox.

More Boompop Benefits For The Rest Of Us

- Learning the unifying building blocks that govern all music.

- Establishing a groove repertoire. Each style interprets rhythm and pocket differently, each style has something vital to offer.

- Prosody and language explored throughout.

- Reading and understanding rhythm, what we call rhythm theory. From long tones, to Quarters, 8ths, 16ths, Triplet rhythms as well as rests.

- Ongoing explorations in audiation—bringing out melodies from inside; borrowing and repurposing from the icons of the past.

- Supplying a non restrictive mindset--we are students of all rhythm, melody, harmony, and style. No borders/no boundaries.

- Improves understanding of the appropriate application of all rhythm and phrasing.

- "The Groove" supplies a useful musical context that supports and inspires practical musical exploration of rhythm, melody, harmony, style, and so much more.

- Versatility--we are inspired by all music. We are exposed to all music.

- Creativity/Originality--being that our musical palet is denser, creative choices are limitless. The combining of seemingly disparate styles in unique ways is what originality is all about.

Boompop is a realistic approach to improvisation that incorporates all styles in a life long learning process. In the process we will learn to adapt to any musical situation. Improvisational skills equate to adaptive skills in Boompop. In Boompop, we improve our improvisational skills more by borrowing from a variety of sources, learning new than any single style (rock, blues, jazz, etc.) could alone. In doing so, adapt intelligently and appropriately to any musical situation. In addition, most modern styles require a degree of adaptability and improvisation in order to master effectively.

For guitar players, Boompop represents a "beyond the tablature" approach to music. Learning an instrument is not just about learning songs. Paradoxically, our approach will teach us to play, feel, breath, and reinterpret within any song, any style, and any sound for those who see it through.

Boompop for Special Needs Application

The Boompop approach has been proven to be an adaptable form of beneficial play for special needs communities. In these encounters, the soft skills learned are of primary importance--how implementing a regular music program to these communities can change lives in and outside of the music realm. We use rhythm and "The One" to address many issues related to individuals with special needs. A creative music approach like Boompop fosters growth in many areas.

The Brain

Its well documented that learning music increases gray matter volume in various regions within the brain. This grey matter deals with the regions of the brain involved in muscle control, memory, emotions, speech, decision making, and sensory perception such as seeing, hearing, and touch, etc. Through music, focus improves significantly. Music is also a useful tool in helping to improve verbal memory and literacy well as.

As musical disciplines go, the study of Boompop merges the creative with the analytical functions of the brain. Music as an outlet for creative, even playful energy, is alive and well in our approach. We don't address the analytical with these communities verbally. Instead, we aim for the experience of the concept, whatever that may be. Lastly, the study of music addresses a variety of senses simultaneously--sight, sound, and touch (tactile stimulation).

Movement & Stress Relief

The act of play reduces stress and anxiety. It's as simple as that. Play lowers the effects of stress, allowing the student to be in the right state of mind to experience and accept relevant cues, communicate more effectively, and learn lessons without the shame normally attributed to growth. The result is a healthier client/student and a happier, more actualized life.

Movement within the musical experience (referred to eurhythmics) is important in the study of Boompop. Music--rhythm, groove, expression, and nuance--is something to be felt physically. This is why movement is so important to serve as a tool to "lock it in" musically. In doing so, we increase blood flow and oxygen to all parts of the body. In addition, group movement releases endorphins that make us feel better, decreasing depression, and increasing confidence and self acceptance, along with an overall improved disposition.

Community

The community aspect of Boompop is referred to as "banding"--establishing relationships, negotiating agendas, communicating, and belonging to something bigger than the individual. The level of connection that occurs when a person plays music with another person is magical. In short, playing music naturally enforces human connection, a sense of belonging, reduces feelings of isolation, improves relationships, as well as fosters teamwork. Studies have shown that social connection improves physical health as well as mental and emotional well-being. On the other hand, low levels of social connection are associated with decline in physical and psychological health as well as a higher likelihood for antisocial behavior that leads to further isolation.

Music & Wellness + The One = Inclusion

In my teachings, I often talk about being on the one. The One is the musical center, the groove and vibe we all create around. It's about being on time, giving, and being in the moment. Playing what is needed for the whole, setting the ego aside. I'm an author, an educator, a musician, a composer and an arranger. I've been working with people and personalities for 30 years. My programs utilize contemporary music of all kinds to achieve bigger goals in various aspects of mental health and overall wellness.

Our aim for the music enrichment program, Music And Wellness, is to utilize music as a tool to achieve non-musical goals. Our classes are led by myself, Rod Goelz, with several mentors in training. The tools we use come from varied, colorful sources. The One is one such tool. I learned about the concept of The One from James Brown, Bootsy Collins, and George Clinton. It was their overriding musical construct that brought musicians together to create great music with a higher purpose--unity! "Funk" in itself, as a dance music, has healing properties that can take one "to church" without entering any building. The One emphasizes the idea that we are all connected, despite our various backgrounds and aptitudes. Our musical choices are felt, and inspired by, the whole of our surroundings. The One teaches many wide-reaching lessons and offers many extra soft-skill benefits to special needs communities.

Connection

"I propose that music is a mechanism for humans to connect with one another. It encourages us to share parts of ourselves through the sounds that are strung together or the singer's prose. When telling our stories or channeling who we are with music, an awareness can develop and a bond can be solidified."

Laura Suval

From the earliest of times, humans communicated and connected through music. This connection is music's biggest gift. In short, connection is what makes us whole. Emma Seppala of Stanford University states, "People who feel more connected to others have lower levels of anxiety and depression. Moreover, studies show they also have higher self-esteem, greater empathy for others, are more trusting and cooperative and, as a consequence, others are more open to trusting and co-operating with them. In other words, social connectedness generates a positive feedback loop of social, emotional, and physical well-being."

Our special needs communities experience The One and human connection at work every time they participate in movement, collective drumming, group singing, or ensemble playing. The resultant energy shift is immediate--bodies loosen, smiles pop, fears subside, players share personal issues and learning in an organic way, in natural, uncoerced conversation.

Expression

"If you can walk you can dance, if you can talk you can sing..."

Zimbabwean Proverb

Music is about freedom of expression. Our classes have had great success in carving out a safe space for students to express themselves. We have helped transition clients who were quiet and uncommunicative into vibrant, singing, chatterboxes. We express ourselves in our talking, singing, instrument work--even the way we move. Each student plays a major role in breaking down barriers. The One is the perfect construct to channel musical expression, energy, and movement.

According to Abbie Sealover, a former Direct Support Professional for K, 31, Music and Wellness was a safe and unassuming space for her to work on how her behavior affects others. Group activities like drumming, dancing, and ensemble work provided opportunities for K to work on non-verbal communication. The open, fun, and playful environment allowed her to expand her rigid thinking and improve dramatically in the areas of adaptability, consideration for others, and working with a team. All which were at one time challenging for her, including her narrow view on what was considered good music. This has all lead to K being able to connect the dots and apply the skills learned in Music and Wellness in everyday life situations. She often says, "Abbie would be so proud of me," which is her way of saying, "I'm proud of me."

Another example: "T is a 62 year old man with an intellectual disability. One of his main challenges in day to day life is communication. It wasn't until I saw T with a guitar and singing that I realized his way of communicating to the world around him was through music. Finding Music and Wellness was a blessing that continues to blossom through all areas of his life. Music offers T a way to connect to his peers and the world around him, as well as gifting him a safe place to express himself in the language most familiar to him. A language so familiar to us all, the language of vibration. This once quiet man has since serenaded the librarian, initiates conversations, and has shown an overall boost in confidence. Music has not only helped T with his confidence, but allows his heart to shine on a daily basis improving his overall quality of life." - Rosanna DiSebastiano - Community Development Instructor

Music and Wellness offers "built-to-suit" programs for a variety of different demographics: Special needs individuals, preschoolers, teens, individuals in recovery, and elderly. Music and the discipline of learning a musical instrument along with the creative act of making music can improve life, learning, and mental health

Negotiation

The act of making music is a series of interactions and negotiations with other humans. In other words, music helps us recognize and respond to social cues. It is a discipline that requires mindfulness and compromise—listening to your fellow music-mates and being sensitive to the sounds, rhythms, and the space created by percussive attack, strum, or shake. The choices made while creating music can open dialogue about topics other than music in a natural way that often leads to personal discoveries. Such discussions can help students see new ways to achieve life goals.

It's important to understand that all people are capable of this type of interaction and discovery on some level. Certainly every person comes with a set of natural abilities and aptitudes. It is also true that each person brings with them personality traits, energy, and abilities that make them unique and vital to the whole ensemble.

Simple/Effective Tasks

The One is the realization that basic tasks done well are vital in the music-making experience. Inclusion in ensembles is a given. An ensemble succeeds through the combined efforts and varying abilities of the members of the ensemble. Since Music and Wellness began, we periodically play in "band" style. The most noticeable change I have seen is in the attitude and body language of our participants. Their energy and their smiles brighten. Learning takes place without the facilitator having to say a word. We learn to compromise, we learn listening, we learn motor skills, but most importantly we learn to adjust our actions to the needs of the people around us. The drummer doesn't need to be a prodigy to keep the steady beat the rest of the group relies on. Similarly, the skills learned in Music and Wellness help individuals with special needs increase their ability to enter the workforce. Throughout our learning sessions, we discover that inclusion is firmly within reach for those with special needs.

In Closing

I've been connected to many of these clients for over two years. Watching them blossom in their expression, experience, and actively take in new information has been wonderful to watch. So very proud of them. My task is to find new ways to open up channels for their betterment.

Who would have expected that the lessons passed down from funk pioneers would have such a wide range of benefits for special needs communities? Music is healing, communication, connection, expression, and negotiation. Music produces smiles and good energy, eases burdens, and provides a template that inspires and opens a space for inclusion. And it does so in the most non-obtrusive, painless way. For our special needs communities, James Brown's "Brand New Bag" is the magic formula for a better life.

Rod Goelz
Biography

Rod Goelz is a musician, published author, and music educator who has gone international with his music and teaching methods. His innovative QuickStart Guitar Method has gotten notice from The Associated Press, who called Rod a "Six-String Surgeon," and earned Rod a Grammy nomination for music education.

A native of York, PA, Rod has been mentoring musicians and creating music for more than 30 years. Rod studied at the famed Berklee College of Music and earned a Bachelor of Arts in Music Industry Studies from Millersville University.

Rod has taught music, guitar, bass, drums, mandolin and ukulele to thousands of musicians and he is credited for his ability in helping beginners realize their goals as well as taking advanced players to the next level of playing. Rod's background and understanding of all styles offers something unique and valuable to every musician. He believes that the best way to learn an instrument is to play with others from the first day. Application brings understanding and motivation. It's this belief that brought about his successful Rock Band Music Program; a program where students learn music, style, technique, arranging, songwriting, marketing, recording all within the context of forming an actual rock band.

Known for his involvement with such diverse bands such as Paradise Movement and American Hollar, Rod is also the founder and leader of Groove Jones, and most recently, Boompop Coalition.

Another defining feature of the Boompop Approach is adaptation through versatility and improvisation. According to Goelz, all styles of music have something musically enriching to offer. No musical taboos and no boundaries. His "Boompop Approach," has won the praise of many as being an alternative improvisational, educational, and musical style.

Rod's most recent venture brings him back to his hometown, as the Head of WAG Music, the contemporary music division of the Weary Arts Group located at Union Lutheran Church. He brings with him his Rock Band, QuickStart Guitar, Boompop, and Music & Wellness Programs along with a host of other learning opportunities for people young and old.

www.ingramcontent.com/pod-product-compliance
Lightning Source LLC
Chambersburg PA
CBHW030830060726

47590CB00004B/1472